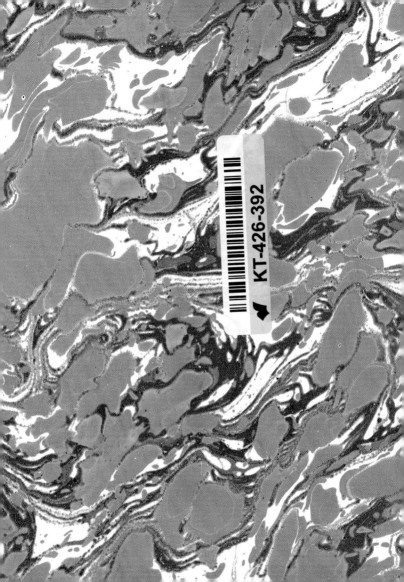
KT-426-392

THE NATIONAL TRUST
Little Library

Salad Herbs

JILL NORMAN

DORLING KINDERSLEY
LONDON

EDITOR GWEN EDMONDS

DESIGNER JOANNA MARTIN

PHOTOGRAPHER DAVE KING

ART DIRECTOR STUART JACKMAN

FIRST PUBLISHED IN GREAT BRITAIN IN 1989 BY
DORLING KINDERSLEY LIMITED
9 HENRIETTA STREET LONDON WC2E 8PS

TEXT COPYRIGHT © 1989 JILL NORMAN
ILLUSTRATION COPYRIGHT © 1989
DORLING KINDERSLEY LIMITED

ALL RIGHTS RESERVED. NO PART OF THIS PUBLICATION
MAY BE REPRODUCED, STORED IN A RETRIEVAL SYSTEM, OR
TRANSMITTED IN ANY FORM OR BY ANY MEANS, ELECTRONIC,
MECHANICAL, PHOTOCOPYING, RECORDING OR OTHERWISE,
WITHOUT THE PRIOR WRITTEN PERMISSION OF THE COPYRIGHT HOLDER.

BRITISH LIBRARY CATALOGUING IN PUBLICATION DATA

NORMAN, JILL
SALAD HERBS.
THE NATIONAL TRUST LITTLE LIBRARY
1. HERBS 2. SALADS
I. TITLE II. SERIES
641.357

ISBN 0-86318-303-4

PRINTED AND BOUND
IN HONG KONG BY IMAGO

CONTENTS

INTRODUCTION

*T*HE HERB GARDENS OF THE PAST, *were
well ordered collections of plants. They supplied
the household with all manner of tonics, medi-
cines, cosmetics and sweet waters, plants for the
still room, for strewing and for decorative use as
well as for the kitchen.*

John Evelyn
1620–1706

*Pot herbs and aromatic herbs were as important as
cultivated salad plants and many more salad herbs came from the
wild. In 1629 John Parkinson, herbalist to Charles I, defined the
composition of a salad as 'the buds and leaves of everything almost that
groweth, as well in the garden as in the fields, and put altogether, that
the taste of the one may amend the rellish of the other'.*

At the end of the century John Evelyn listed some seventy plants that
could be used in salads. These could be eaten raw or blanched,
occasionally preserved or candied, alone or in a compound salad. He
also gave instructions about dressing salads. He considered the olive oil
of Lucca in Tuscany to be the best. His advice is very similar to that of
the French poet Ronsard, more than a hundred years earlier, who wrote
of going out to gather salad herbs, washing them in the fountain, then
seasoning them with salt, rose-flavoured vinegar and oil from
Provence. The advice holds good: oil, vinegar and salt, perhaps with the
addition of some pepper, still make the best dressing for a green salad.
A vegetable salad may require a stronger flavouring such as a mustard
or a mayonnaise dressing.

The range of oils and flavoured vinegars for dressings is now very
wide and I hope that some of the old salad sauces based on cream and

milk may become popular again. Rose water and orange-flower water make a pleasant dressing on occasion, too. Green salads should be dressed just before they are served so that they stay fresh and crisp; vegetable salads should be prepared an hour or so before serving so that the dressing penetrates and flavours the vegetables. A mixed salad, like that mentioned by Park-inson, could be a very grand affair. Old cookery books describe in detail how to present a grand composed salad to be pleasing to all the senses: the aromatic flavours of tarragon, chives and chervil would be balanced by blander purslane, lettuce or corn salad, and the visual appeal would be enhanced by flowers such as borage, marigold, violets or roses. We are fortunate that after a long lapse many of the

Title page of Gerard's Herball 1633 edition

past are available again. They can be bought or grown quite easily, and greatly enhance our salads and many other dishes.

The recipes in this book are for salads, light soups and other dishes in which the flavour of the fresh herbs can be appreciated. Unless you are addicted to a particular herb, it is best not to increase quantities without trying the recipe first because a dominant flavour of one herb can be unpleasant. Always use fresh herbs; with few exceptions salad herbs do not dry well, and certainly when dried their taste is very different and in my opinion only suited to cooked dishes.

B A S I L

$\mathcal{B}$ASIL *is a member of the mint family. It grows throughout the tropics, and is the most strongly-flavoured herb that will grow in rather cool climates. From its native India it was brought to the Middle East. The ancient Greeks knew it and Virgil mentions it, but it did not reach western Europe until the 16th century, and the New World much later. The strong spicy smell of well-established plants pervades the garden in summer and if you walk through a Greek village the air is filled with the 'excellent, pleasant sweet scent' (as Parkinson called it) from the pots of basil on every wall and window-sill.*

Sweet, common or Genovese basil (*Ocimum basilicum*) is the larger-leaved and stronger-flavoured variety; it will grow well in a temperate climate in good summers (or under glass).

It is best to let it bush by pinching out the centre when some 6 inches (15 cm) high, and then take care to keep it from flowering. Bush or Greek basil (*Ocimum minimum*) grows in small-leaved bushes to no more than 6–8 inches (15–20 cm) compared to sweet basil's 18–24 inches (45–60 cm). Lettuce basil has large floppy leaves while ruffles basil has

Ocimum minimum

Ocimum
basilicum

'Faire basil
desireth it may
be her lot to
growe as the
gilliflower, trim
in a pot'
Thomas Tusser,
500 points of Husbandry,
1573

crinkly ones; both look good in
a salad (as do the purple
varieties, which are otherwise a
bit disappointing).

All basils need a light rich soil
and as much sun as they can get.
Although not strictly annual
it is hard to keep through
the winter. Bush basil is the
sturdier variety; pagoda basil,
the sacred *tulsi* of Hindu
temples, the most fragile.
Basil has a rich, mildly peppery
flavour with a hint of mint and
cloves. It blends well with garlic
and lemon. Too often associated
only with pesto or with
tomatoes, pungent basil is
equally good with eggs and in
potato, bean or rice salads,
or used whole in mixed and
green salads. Sprigs of basil
make an aromatic garnish,
as do the edible flowers.
Basil is also one of the
great cooking herbs,
essential in Mediterra-
nean, Indian and Thai
food. As a flavouring
for vinegar or oil basil
has few equals.

O. Basilicum Purpurascens

BORAGE

*B*ORAGO OFFICINALIS *is a common wild herb in southern Europe which was taken northwards by the Roman legions, and is now found on chalky soils in many countries.*

Borage is an annual plant which can be grown from seed. It should be sown in late spring or early autumn, in any well-drained soil, but it likes some chalk or sand. Thinned to about 15 inches (40 cm) rather than planted out, it will reach up to 3 feet (90 cm) in height, and seeds itself quite readily. It is valuable in the garden for attracting bees and so furthering pollination. The beautiful deep blue flowers with their dramatic black centres were once a favourite pattern in needlework. They still add edible glamour to salads or can be candied for use on cakes. The young leaves have a fresh flavour, not unlike cucumber, and are traditionally used in drinks such as Pimms and other cups.

Borage can also be cooked like sorrel and used as a flavourful purée to add colour to sauces and to stuffings for ravioli and other dishes. In salads the young grey-green leaves improve not just the taste but also the appearance, especially of potato salad. Its close relative comfrey (*Symphytum officinale*) can often serve as a substitute.

Borago officinalis

CHERVIL

*A*NTHRISCUS CEREFOLIUM, *our garden chervil, is native to the Middle East and the south of the Soviet Union. The Romans, once again, brought it west. In French cooking it has gained the place which parsley has in the English-speaking world.*

It is an annual which is easy to grow from seed in light moist soil. The plant will reach 2 feet (50 cm), but if kept low by cutting back it will produce better leaves. These fragile-looking leaves are of a whitish green, sometimes tinged with red in summer. Chervil quickly runs to seed, after which, like most herbs, it is well past its best. To keep a good supply it is advisable to sow at intervals of a few weeks.

Chervil has a delicate flavour, with a hint of anise. It is an essential ingredient in *fines herbes*, goes well with eggs, and is a good flavouring for soups, for salads based on potato or rice, and for salad dressings. It must be used quite lavishly, and chopped at the last minute for it soon loses its aroma.

Anthriscus cerefolium

CHIVES

*A*LLIUM SCHOENOPRASUM *is the smallest member of the onion family. It grows in the temperate and northern parts of Europe, Asia and America, and is widely cultivated.*

A hardy perennial which grows in dense clumps to about 10 inches (25 cm), it can be propagated from seed or by division into smaller clumps. The plants should be cropped severely several times during the season, they require a light soil, good light and much water. The grass-like, round and hollow leaves are only used fresh. Chopped up fine, they enhance omelettes and other egg dishes, white cheese, potatoes, soup and all manner of other foods with their light but spicy onion flavour. Chives are one of the classic *fines herbes* and are essential to many herb sauces.

The pretty mauve, or pink, flowers make the plant useful as an edging. The flowers, too, can be used in salads. Chinese chives (*Allium tuberosum*) have flat leaves and white flowers.

Allium schoenoprasum.
Allium tuberosum.

CORNSALAD

*V*ALERIANELLA OLITORIA, *also* VALERIANELLA LOCUSTA, *and popularly known as lamb's lettuce, is a common weed now little cultivated, but rightly popular in France (where it is called mâche), in Germany, and in the eastern states of America.*

Corn salad is an annual plant with elongated bright-green leaves, which survives even under snow. It can be grown from seed at almost any time, in firm fairly rich soil. The drills should be about 4 inches (10 cm) apart and the seedlings will need

thinning to the same distance between plants. The thinnings can be used as a first harvest. In a few weeks the plants will attain their full growth, about 6 inches (15 cm). Do not let them flower or grow too old, for the leaves soon get tough and a little bitter.

Young leaves have a pleasant, pungent taste. They can be used as a salad in their own right. They also make a fine garnish for a variety of pungent foods, from radishes to Roquefort.

Valerianella olitoria

'*The tops and leaves are a sallet of themselves, seasonably eaten with other salleting, the whole winter long, and early spring.*' *Thus John Evelyn in his 'discourse of sallets', the Acetaria of 1699.*

CRESS

*W*ATERCRESS (NASTURTIUM OFFICINALE) *grows wild in most parts of the world but since the 19th century several varieties have been widely cultivated in special beds. A bed may yield as many as ten crops a year as long as there is a steady supply of clean water.*

Watercress is an aquatic perennial. It can be propagated at any time by cuttings rooted in water. If grown in rich moist garden soil its taste will be stronger. Its 'hot', peppery taste makes it useful in salads but it can be cooked and makes good soup. Walnut oil and lemon juice are its best dressing.

Nasturtium officinale

Lepidium sativum

Garden cress (*Lepidium sativum*) originated in Persia and *Sinapis alba*, the white mustard of 'mustard and cress', around the Mediterranean. Both grow wild in Europe and North America. Both are annuals, easy to grow from broadcast seed or in trays on thin soil, even on a piece of moist cloth. Cress germinates more quickly and in mixed trays should be sown three days after mustard. Both are cut when less than 2 inches (5 cm), about a fortnight after sowing the cress.

DANDELION

TARAXACUM OFFICINALE is a native of the temperate zones of Asia and Europe which now grows profusely in North America as well. In France and the western United States it is cultivated to a form much like broad-leaved endive and blanched in the same way.

Dandelions are perennials. They grow on a long tap-root and can be grown from seed in late spring, but many gardeners already have more than they know what to do with. It is easy to make even the unwanted plants useful. Tie the leaves loosely and cover the plant, where it grows, with a plant pot. After about a week of this blanching the leaves will have lost much of their bitterness. Unblanched leaves are only good when very young, eaten with hot bacon. After flowering they get very bitter and blanching is essential, or they can be cooked and eaten with butter, lemon juice and a little nutmeg.

Taraxacum officinale

13

DILL

*A*NETHUM GRAVEOLENS *is particularly popular in Scandinavia and Russia, and also in Canada: in the colder northern climes it provides a much-needed reminder of sun and summer, a touch of pungent freshness.*

Dill is an annual, easily grown from seed; similar to fennel in appearance but with finer leaves and seldom as much as 3 feet (90 cm) high. Fennel and dill should be grown well apart or the more delicate dill will be swamped.

Fragrant, with a delicate but persistent flavour, dill goes well with sour cream or yoghurt, cucumber, egg and fish dishes, rice salads, even boiled potatoes. Parkinson noted that dill *'is also put among pickled cowcumbers, giving unto the cold fruit a pretty spicie taste or rellish'*.

Fresh dill is never used for cooking, unless added at the last minute, for it quickly loses its flavour when heated. On the other hand, unlike most salad herbs dill will keep some of its flavour if dried or frozen.

Anethum graveolens

FENNEL

*S*WEET FENNEL (FOENICULUM VULGARE) *has a strong anise flavour and is a native of southern Europe. It now grows almost everywhere but in the tropics. Florence fennel is a vegetable variety in which the swollen bases of the succulent stems grow bulblike. Its flavour is more delicate than that of ordinary fennel and it makes excellent salads, either with other herbs or mixed with salad vegetables. It goes well with cheese and it can be braised.*

Florence fennel

Foeniculum vulgare

Both fennels are hardy perennials, easily grown from seed. Sweet fennel plants will reach heights of 3–6 feet (1–2 m), but to maintain a good supply of leaves it is better to keep them lower. If left unchecked, they will bear large umbels of yellow flowers from mid-summer and seed themselves profusely.

Florence fennel is less easy to rear and needs more attention. It likes a rich soil and when the bases swell they need covering with earth.

Fennel stalks dry successfully and in Provençal cooking are flamed to impart their flavour to grilled sea bass or mullet.

GARLIC

*A*LLIUM SATIVUM *is one of the oldest cultivated plants, and a greatly venerated one. Although growing wild in central Asia, its natural habitat is thought to have been the Mediterranean. The Roman legions brought it to Britain, and later Italian emigrants have taken it all over the world.*

Garlic is a perennial bulb made up of a cluster of cloves. The plant looks much like the onion plant. It reaches a height of 15 inches (40 cm).

Traditionally the cleaned bulbs are plaited for storage by their long dry leaves.

'Eat no onions nor garlic, for we are to utter sweet breath'

Bottom admonished his players (A Midsummer Night's Dream IV:2) Most of garlic's bad reputation rests on misuse. Cooked garlic leaves no trace on the breath, but fried too hot it gets acrid. Raw garlic should be chopped fine.

Allium sativum

P A R S L E Y

*P*ETROSELINUM CRISPUM *is a native of the eastern
Mediterranean which is now found in many temperate
regions. The variety* Petroselinum sativum, *called Italian Parsley
(or, in the U.S., flat) came from Italy, probably in the 15th century.
It is hardier and stronger in taste then the curly sort which has become
the most common beyond the Mediter –   ranean region.*

Parsley is a biennial grown
from seed. Soak the seeds
overnight, or steep in boiling
water to speed up germination.
Parsley needs a well-forked
bed and likes light and
moisture.

Petroselinum crispum

*Petroselinum
sativum*

In Anglo-Saxon   cooking parsley
is the universal   herb, often
used as mere decoration. Crisp fresh
parsley enhances almost any
dish or salad, especially since
it will bring out the flavour
of other herbs. It survives
cooking, even frying – fried
parsley, in fact, is to be
relished as a vegetable or as
a garnish for fried fish.

PURSLANE

*P*ORTULACA OLERACEA *grows wild throughout much of
the world, but its region of origin remains unknown. The
cultivated sorts were first developed in the Middle East. In Mexico and
the southern United States purslane (also commonly called pigweed,
as are many similar herbs) was a staple Indian food.*

It is a sprawling annual which prefers a dry sandy soil but needs frequent watering and a fair amount of sun. It is best to harvest young shoots of no more than 2–3 inches (5–7 cm), and the plants will produce several crops if cut well back.

Portulaca oleracea

The thick fleshy leaves have a sharp fresh taste – *'eminently moist and cooling'* according to Evelyn. They are excellent in salads: Middle Eastern *fattoush* and Provençal *mesclun* are not complete without them. They can also be cooked or pickled in salt and vinegar.

Claytonia (*C. perfoliata*) or winter purslane is a pretty, mild – flavoured annual. It is a useful salad herb year round, but especially welcome in winter.

Claytonia perfoliata

R O C K E T

Eruca sativa is native to western Asia and southern Europe. It grows as a weed in Britain, where it was introduced by the Romans, and in North America, where it is also known as arugula. Rocket was very popular through the Middle Ages and until the late 18th century, but it is no longer much cultivated outside southern France and Italy. It is well worth a revival in the garden, as its taste is quite unlike that of any other salad herb.

Rocket is an annual. It can be grown from seed, in spring or autumn, and gives the best results when raised quickly in rich moist soil. It will be ready for use within eight weeks, and will stand repeated cutting. Garden varieties have creamy flowers, often with a streak of purple.

Rocket has a very distinctive, pleasantly pungent taste ('*hot and dry*' says Evelyn) which makes an interesting contribution to mixed green salads, especially as a contrast with soft lettuce.

Eruca sativa

SALAD BURNET

*P*OTERIUM SANGUISORBA *is a European garden herb. It was much loved in Elizabethan England and taken to the New World from there.*

It is a small perennial, at most a foot (30 cm) high, which grows wild on chalky soils. Flower stems are best removed to encourage leaf growth through the summer. Strong plants often last well into winter, surviving early snow. The small finely toothed leaves are green on the upper side and greyish underneath. Their taste is reminiscent of cucumber, in fact the whole plant *'doth smell something like a melon, or cucumber'* thought Gerard. *(The Herball, 1633).*

In mixed green salads both its taste and its looks make a valuable contribution. In cooling summer drinks it may be used instead of borage.

Poterium sanguisorba

Burnet combines well with tarragon and rosemary for herb butters, or with mint for sauces.

SWEET CICELY

M YRRHIS ODORATA, *also known as sweet or anise chervil, grows wild in northern Europe, including parts of England and Scotland. In North America it is common in a variant called* Osmorhiza longistylis.

Sweet cicely is a stout perennial. It can be grown from seed, or by root division. It will grow, very slowly, to a good 3 feet (nearly a metre) but can easily be kept lower for scented borders. Its feathery leaves, bright green up top but pale underneath, and its umbels of white flowers are quite decorative. Cicely prefers shade. It lasts from early spring well into winter but it seeds quickly and freely, after which the leaves have little strength.

Myrrhis odorata

All parts of the plant can be eaten. The leaves and hollow stems, with the flavour of anise, are used in salads, including fruit salads. The tap-root when boiled, or the seeds make an interesting salad with just a simple dressing.

The stems can also be candied and used like angelica. Cicely makes a useful sugar substitute in conserves and fruit dishes, and is often used to sweeten cream. It does not lose its flavour in cooking.

TARRAGON

*A*RTEMISIA DRACUNCULUS, *a native of central Asia, was brought to Spain by the Moors – the name derives from Arabic* tarkhun. *It has been an important ingredient in French cooking since the 16th century, and although slower to gain recognition elsewhere, it is now cultivated throughout Europe and North America.*

The 'real' (French) tarragon is a bushy perennial which needs a well-drained sandy soil. It likes some peat and a fair amount of

Artemisia dracunculus

sun. Grown from spring cuttings or by root division, French tarragon will reach some 2–3 feet (60–90 cm). In winter it needs cutting back and covering. Every few years a tarragon bed must be renewed or the plants will grow lanky and their flavour diminish.

Russian tarragon (*A. dracunculoides* or *redowskii*) is an inferior variety. Its flavour is said to improve with plant age, but even so it is never in the same class as the French.

Tarragon is an essential component of *fines herbes*. Its tangy and slightly bitter taste is much liked in egg dishes, cream soups and with roast poultry, in mustard or as tarragon vinegar. Béarnaise and tartare sauce depend on it. Tarragon keeps its flavour well when dried.

OCCASIONAL
SALAD HERBS

*T*HE YOUNG LEAVES *of spinach, sorrel, lovage, hyssop and lemon balm may be used to enliven a salad.*

Wood
Sorrel

Lemon
balm

Sorrel

Hyssop

Recipes

All recipes are for 4,
but some (such as Gravad Lax)
will serve more

CUCUMBER AND BORAGE SOUP

2 cucumbers, peeled, seeded and
chopped
3 spring onions, chopped
a large handful young borage leaves
½ pint/300 ml cold consommé
½ pint/300 ml yoghurt
¼ pint/150 ml double cream
salt and pepper
lemon juice (optional)

Put the cucumber, onion and half the borage leaves into a processor or blender and work to a purée. Transfer the purée to a large bowl or tureen and stir in the consommé. Whisk together the yoghurt and cream and add to the cucumber mixture. Taste, and season with salt and pepper and a few drops of lemon juice if you wish.

Chill thoroughly. Chop the remaining borage leaves finely and sprinkle over the soup just before serving. If you have a few borage flowers, float them on the surface.

ALMOND AND GARLIC
SOUP WITH GRAPES

This is a version of Andalusian gazpacho called *ajo blanco*.

4 oz/125 g blanched almonds
4 large cloves garlic
salt
2 thick slices white bread, crusts removed
2 tablespoons olive oil
2 teaspoons wine vinegar
about 1½ pints/900 ml water
8 oz/250 g white grapes
4 ice cubes

Crush the almonds and garlic together with some salt. This may be done in a blender or a mortar. Add small pieces of bread and the oil and continue to blend, then add the vinegar. Add enough water to achieve a smooth milky consistency. Chill the soup.

Unless the grapes are the small seedless variety, cut them in half and remove the pips. To serve, pour the soup into a tureen and add the ice cubes and grapes.

ROCKET, LEEK AND
POTATO SOUP

1 lb/500 g potatoes
2 leeks
1¼ pints/750 ml water
salt and pepper
2 large handfuls of rocket leaves
¼ pint/150 ml cream

Cut the potatoes into small cubes, slice the white part of the leeks thinly and put the vegetables into a pan of salted water. Bring to the boil and then simmer for about 15 minutes, until the vegetables are soft. Put the soup through a vegetable mill or a sieve. Don't use a blender or processor, it will give the potatoes a glue-like texture.

Return the soup to the pan Chop the rocket leaves roughly, and add them to the soup. Stir in the cream, taste for seasoning and simmer gently for 5 minutes.

Serve hot with croûtons. To serve cold, add another ¼ pint/150 ml cream, chill and garnish with more chopped rocket.

OKROSHKA

A western interpretation of a
popular cold soup from Russia.

2 hard-boiled eggs
2 teaspoons Dijon mustard
¼ pint/150 ml sour cream
salt, pepper
1 pint/600 ml plain yoghurt
1 pint/600 ml soda water
3 spring onions, chopped
6 radishes, sliced
1 medium cucumber, chopped
2 small pickled cucumbers, chopped
1 tablespoon chopped chives
1 tablespoon chopped parsley
2 tablespoons chopped dill
12 oz/375 g cooked, shelled prawns

Chop the egg whites and put
them to one side. Mash the
yolks with the mustard, then
stir in the sour cream and
season with salt and pepper.
Beat in the yoghurt slowly, then
the soda water, until all is well
blended. Pour the soup into a
large bowl or tureen and add
the vegetables, herbs and
prawns. Chill the soup for at
least an hour, taste for
seasoning and add the chopped
egg white just before serving.

CHERVIL SOUP

2 oz/50 g butter
2 tablespoons flour
2 pints/1.2 litres hot chicken stock
salt and pepper
2 oz/50 g chervil, finely chopped
2 egg yolks
4 tablespoons cream

Melt the butter in a heavy pan,
stir in the flour to make a roux
then gradually add the stock,
stirring well. Season with salt
and pepper and let the soup
simmer for 10 minutes.
Warm a soup tureen and put in
the chervil, egg yolks and
cream. Whisk them together
briefly then pour in the hot
soup, a little at a time, stirring
to blend thoroughly.
Serve at once.

$\mathcal{F}$ISH SALAD

8 oz/250 g monkfish, without bone
8 oz/250 g lemon sole
4 scallops
small lettuce leaves and other non-bitter small salad greens
sprigs of sweet cicely
vinaigrette made with 4 tablespoons olive oil, 1½ tablespoons lemon juice, salt and pepper

Cut the monkfish and sole diagonally into thin slices. Detach the corals from the scallops and slice the scallops in half.
Set water to boil in a steamer and steam the monkfish until opaque, about 3–4 minutes. The sole and scallops will take slightly less time, 2–3 minutes, and the corals 1–2 minutes. (Steam them separately or add the sole and scallops while the monkfish is cooking.)
Remove the fish from the steamer and allow to cool. Arrange the salad greens on 4 plates and distribute the fish and scallops over them. Dress with the vinaigrette and decorate with small sprays of sweet cicely leaves and top each plate with a coral.

$\mathcal{B}$ROAD BEAN, BASIL AND MUSHROOM SALAD

2 lb/1 kg broad beans (to give about 1 lb/500 g shelled beans)
4 oz/125 g button mushrooms
2–3 spring onions
2 tablespoons chopped basil
5 tablespoons olive oil
2 tablespoons lemon juice
salt and pepper

Small, young beans are best for this salad, but larger ones can be used if you take off the skins after cooking. Boil the beans until tender and drain well.
Wipe the mushrooms, leave whole if they are very small, or cut them in half. Chop the onions finely, including some of the green part.
Put all the vegetables and the basil in a bowl, make a dressing with the oil, lemon juice, salt and pepper and pour it over the vegetables. Toss the salad well and leave to marinate for 2–3 hours (not in the refrigerator) before serving.

FRENCH BEAN SALAD

1 lb/500 g small French beans
6 tablespoons of a variety of chopped
herbs such as chervil, chives,
parsley, salad burnet, tarragon
5 tablespoons olive oil
2 tablespoons herb vinegar (p. 38)
salt, pepper
anchovy fillets (optional)

Top and tail the beans and cook them in boiling salted water until just tender. Drain the beans and plunge them into a bowl of cold water. Drain again. When quite dry put the beans into a salad bowl, sprinkle the mixed herbs over them and dress with a vinaigrette made with the olive oil, vinegar, salt and pepper. Garnish with the anchovies, if you wish, and serve.

ROCKET AND CORN SALAD WITH PEARS

Choose *2 ripe, firm Comice or Williams' pears*. Peel, core and slice them and paint the sides with *lemon juice* so they don't discolour. Arrange some rocket and corn salad leaves in a shallow bowl and lay the slices of pear on top. Make a dressing with *walnut oil*, more *lemon juice* and a little *salt and pepper*. Spoon it over the salad, scatter over a handful of walnut halves and serve at once.

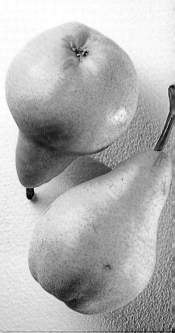

TABBOULEH

2 oz/50 g burghul (cracked wheat)
1 bunch spring onions, chopped
2 tomatoes, peeled, seeded and
chopped
lettuce leaves
2 large bunches flat leafed parsley,
chopped
5 tablespoons chopped mint leaves
6 tablespoons olive oil
juice of 1 lemon, or more to taste
salt and pepper

Soak the burghul in cold water for 20 minutes then drain and press out the excess water. Add the onion to the burghul and mix thoroughly. Season with salt and pepper and stir in the parsley, mint and tomato. Stir in the olive oil and enough lemon juice to give a tart flavour. Serve on a platter lined with lettuce leaves or use the leaves as a scoop to pick up the tabbouleh.

WATERCRESS AND ORANGE SALAD

2 bunches watercress
2 oranges
2 oz/50 g broken walnuts or
1 oz/25 g toasted pine nuts
2 tablespoons sesame oil
1 tablespoon sunflower oil
2 teaspoons rice vinegar
salt and pepper

Remove any long stalks from the watercress. Peel the oranges, remove any pith and separate into segments. Arrange the cress and oranges in a salad bowl, and sprinkle over the nuts. Make a dressing with the oil and vinegar and a little salt and pepper. Pour over the salad and serve.

FENNEL SALAD

This is one of the easiest and best salads, particularly at the end of a substantial meal. Take *2 or 3 bulbs of fennel*, cut off the tops and a thick slice from the bottom. Remove the tough outer leaves. Cut the fennel into very thin slices and arrange them on a platter. Dress with *salt, black pepper* and lots of good *olive oil*.

If you want to vary the salad add *thin slices of orange* with all peel, pith and pips removed and a few *black olives*. Another possibility is *a small red pepper* cut into thin strips and added to the fennel.

PURSLANE, POTATO AND GOAT'S CHEESE SALAD

1 small cucumber
12 tiny new potatoes
1 bunch purslane
2 small goat's cheeses
green olives
olive oil
chive (p. 38) or wine vinegar
salt and pepper

Cut the cucumber in half lengthways, remove the seeds and cut it into strips. Put the strips in a colander, sprinkle with salt, and leave for an hour.

Boil or steam the potatoes and slice them. Cut the goat's cheese into strips. Pick over the purslane, discarding stalks. Dry the cucumber and arrange the vegetables in a salad bowl or on individual plates. Dress with oil, vinegar, black pepper, and a little salt if necessary. Garnish the salad with the strips of cheese and the olives and serve at once.

CORN SALAD WITH QUAIL'S EGGS

12 quail's eggs
2 bunches corn salad
4 oz/125 g coppa salami cut into thin strips
olive oil
black pepper

Cook the quail's eggs and shell them or not as you wish, but cut them in half. Place the corn salad on individual plates with the ham and dress with olive oil and black pepper. Add the quail's eggs and serve.

GREEN RICE SALAD

4 oz/125 g long grain rice
1 small onion, chopped finely
salt
3 tablespoons olive oil
4 handfuls of assorted chopped herbs
1 tablespoon tarragon vinegar
chive flowers, bergamot flowers,
nasturtiums or marigolds for
garnish

Put the rice in a large bowl,
pour boiling water over it, stir
and leave for 5 minutes. Then
drain and rinse in cold water.
Bring ¼ pint/150 ml salted
water to the boil, put in the rice,
bring to the boil again and turn
down to the lowest possible
simmer. Cover the pan and
leave for 10 minutes. By this
time all the water should be
absorbed and small holes should
have formed in the surface of
the rice. Remove the pan from
the heat. Add 2 tablespoons oil
and cover tightly again and
leave for 10 minutes. The rice
should still be firm and have a
bite to it.

Turn out the rice into a large
bowl using a big wooden fork.
Allow it to cool, then put the
onion and herbs into the bowl
and stir them in, still using the
fork.

Season with 1 more tablespoon
olive oil, 1 tablespoon tarragon
vinegar and black pepper.

Decorate the salad with a few
flowers and serve.

GREEN SALAD WITH SOUR CREAM SAUCE

1 or 2 lettuce hearts
an assortment of young salad leaves
– rocket, sorrel, spinach, corn salad,
cress, purslane, dandelion
8 tablespoons sour cream
3 hard-boiled eggs
salt, pepper
2 teaspoons wine vinegar
1 tablespoon each chopped chervil,
fennel and tarragon

Put the salad greens in a bowl.
Make the dressing by mashing
the egg yolks and blending them
with the cream. Season with
salt, pepper and vinegar and
strain through a sieve. Add the
chopped herbs to the dressing
and pour over salad. Garnish
with chopped egg white.

FINES HERBES

A combination of three (hence in Italian *verdure tritate*) or more finely chopped herbs used to flavour many dishes and occasionally salads.

The classic French *fines herbes* are chervil, parsley, tarragon, chives and thyme.

Beyond the confines of classic French cooking the selection varies considerably, depending both on the dish to be garnished and on local availability or preference.

Basil will be an essential part of *fines herbes* in Italy or the Provence, dill in the combinations used in Scandinavia, Germany and Hungary.

Mint is much liked in similar herb mixtures used in the Middle East and Greece.

Other herbs found in adaptations of the *fines herbes* formula include savory, lemon thyme, burnet, hyssop, purslane, marjoram, celery, fennel, borage, even garden cress. Obviously, there is ample scope for the expression of individual taste and ingenuity.

HERB SALADS

Until well into the 19th century herbs meant almost any small leafy vegetable. Many plants not thought of today as herbs or salad vegetables were routinely used in the kitchen. In his *Acetaria* (1699) John Evelyn lists more than seventy plants, both wild and cultivated, that were considered suitable for salads. He includes alexanders, long forgotten but still easy to find growing wild, all sorts of flowers, hops, shredded orange and lemon peel and samphire, both raw and pickled.

There seems to be a revival of interest in salad vegetables and several kinds of chicory, curly endive, red lollo lettuce, oak leaf and corn salad are now readily available from supermarkets and greengrocers.

You can make your salad livelier still by adding young dandelion leaves, young spinach, sorrel or nasturtium, leaves, rocket, young borage, sweet cicely, lovage or lemon balm leaves, hyssop, salad burnet, chopped mint, purslane, tarragon, orach. Garnish it with herb flowers, marigolds, nasturtiums.

Dress a herb salad with *virgin olive oil* or *walnut oil* and *sherry* or *herb vinegar* (p. 38) and garnish it with *chapons*. For the chapons crush *a clove of garlic* with *a little salt* and mix it with *2–3 tbs of olive oil*. Brush *2 or 3 thick slices of bread* with the oil on both sides and place under a low grill until brown on both sides. Brush with more oil as necessary. Cube the bread and distribute the chapons over the salad.

MESCLUN

Mesclun is a dialect word from Nice meaning a mixture of salad herbs. It may include rocket, dandelion leaves, corn salad, red chicory, purslane, young lettuce, burnet, watercress, curly endive and chervil. Dress mesclun with olive oil.

CUCUMBER SALAD

2 cucumbers
4 tablespoons sour cream
3 tablespoons chopped chervil
salt and pepper

Peel the cucumber, cut them in half lengthways and remove the seeds. Slice the cucumbers as finely as possible, put the slices in a colander set over a deep plate and sprinkle thickly with salt. Leave the cucumber to drain for at least an hour. Rinse, then press the slices with your hand to extract as much water as possible and dry them on a clean cloth.

Stir the chervil and some freshly ground pepper into the cream and mix in the cucumber. Taste for seasoning and serve chilled. Dill or chives may be used instead of chervil.

NEW POTATOES WITH BASIL AND CHIVE SAUCE

1½ lb/750 g small new potatoes
1 oz/25 g butter
1 tablespoon olive oil
8–10 basil leaves, chopped
2 tablespoons chopped chives
¼ pint/150 ml double cream
salt, pepper

Boil the potatoes in salted water until just tender, then drain and cut them in half. Heat the oil and butter in a sauté pan, put in the basil and cook gently for a few minutes, crushing the basil to release its flavour. Add the potatoes and cook fairly briskly, shaking the pan, until they start to brown. Sprinkle the chives over them and pour in the cream. Season with salt and pepper and simmer gently, shaking the pan occasionally, until the sauce thickens (about 10 minutes).

If you have basil preserved in oil, both the leaves and the oil are good in this dish.

Gravad Lax

Marinated salmon from Sweden that is excellent as an hors d'oeuvre with wholemeal or dark rye bread and a herb and mustard sauce.

2–3 lb/1–1.5 kg piece of salmon, boned
3 tablespoons sea salt
1 tablespoon sugar
2 teaspoons coarsely ground black pepper
a large bunch of dill

Cut the salmon into 2 fillets, remove all visible bones, but leave the skin on. Combine the salt, sugar and black pepper and rub this well in to the flesh of each piece. Put several sprigs of dill in a dish just large enough to take the salmon. Put in one piece, skin side down and scatter any remains of the salt mixture over it. Cover with a layer of dill, then put the other fillet, flesh side down, on top of the first. Put more dill on top. Put a weighted board on top and leave in the refrigerator for 48 hours. Turn the fish over 3 times and baste with any brine.

To serve the salmon, slice it very thinly on the slant. The salmon will keep for up to a week, but will start to get dry.

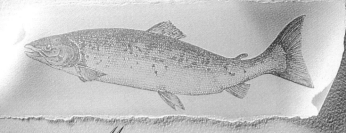

Mustard Sauce

Combine *2 tablespoons of good French mustard* with *½ teaspoon powdered mustard, tablespoon sugar, 2 tablespoons lemon juice* and *3 fl oz/75 ml oil.* When the sauce is well blended, stir in *3 tablespoons of chopped dill.*

BAKED EGGS WITH TARRAGON

4 eggs
40 g/1½ oz butter
8 tablespoons double cream
1½ tablespoons finely chopped
tarragon leaves
salt and pepper

Set the oven at 180°C/350°F/ gas 4 and heat 4 lightly buttered ramekin dishes for a few minutes. Warm the cream, then sprinkle some tarragon in each ramekin and spoon in a little cream. Break an egg into each dish, season with salt and pepper and spoon in some more cream. Top each ramekin with a knob of butter and put them in a bain-marie in the oven for 8–10 minutes until the whites are set and the yolks still soft.

AIOLI

Aioli is a garlic mayonaise from Provence. It is served with crisp raw vegetables, boiled new potatoes, hard-boiled eggs, salt cod or, for a *grand aioli*, a combination of all of these.

4–6 large cloves garlic
salt
2 egg yolks
½ pint/300 ml olive oil
juice of 1 lemon

Pound the garlic and a very little salt to a paste in a mortar. Now, if you intend to continue making the sauce by hand, add the egg yolks and beat until pale. Otherwise, combine the crushed garlic and the yolks in a food processor. Pour in the oil in a thin thread, while turning the pestle, or processing. After adding 3–4 tablespoons of oil, stir in the lemon juice and a teaspoon of warm water. Continue to add oil, little by little, until the mixture thickens again. Add another teaspoon of water and add more oil in a thin stream. Continue in this way until you have used all the oil. When it is ready the aioli should be very thick.

If the oil separates out beat another yolk with a few drops of lemon juice and add the curdled sauce a teaspoon at a time, beating vigorously.

Skordalia

A Greek garlic sauce to serve with boiled potatoes, fried vegetables or fish.

3–4 cloves garlic
salt
6–8 thick slices white bread
3 tablespoons wine vinegar
¼ pint/150 ml olive oil

Mash the garlic with a little salt in a mortar. Cut the crusts from the bread and soak in a little cold water. Squeeze out the surplus water and add the bread to the garlic in the mortar or put both in a food processor. Blend, adding the vinegar a little at a time, until the mixture is smooth. Add the oil gradually, mixing it in to the bread and garlic until it is all absorbed and you have a fairly thick creamy sauce. If it is too thick add a little water at the end.

Pesto

Put *2 good handfuls of basil leaves* into a food processor or a mortar. Add *2 cloves of garlic* crushed with a little *salt* and *1 oz/25 g pine nuts* and process or crush to a paste with a pestle. Now add *1 oz/25 g grated Pecorino* or *Parmesan cheese* and amalgamate with the *basil* mixture. With the processor running or while beating with the pestle, trickle in the *olive oil*, as if making mayonnaise. You will need about *4 or 5 tablespoons* altogether.

The finished sauce should have the consistency of mayonnaise.

Serve it at room temperature with pasta or green vegetables or baked or poached fish.

BASIL PRESERVED IN OLIVE OIL

Put *a large handful of basil leaves* into a glass jar and cover with *olive oil*. Leave the jar in the cupboard for a month and then the basil is ready to use. The oil will have taken the flavour of the basil and gives a distinct aroma of basil to any dish it is used in. Basil preserved in this way is perfect for making pesto.

HERB VINEGAR

Herb vinegars are easy to make and are useful for dressings, sauces and marinades. Use fresh herbs picked early in the day before the sun draws out the aromatic oils, and wine or cider vinegar, or oriental rice vinegar. Tarragon, basil, dill and chives all make excellent vinegars, or try a combination of herbs such as basil, borage, chives and parsley.

Fill a large glass jar with herb sprigs or leaves (if you use chives cut them up) and cover with vinegar. Quantities are approximately *2 oz/50 g of the herb* to *1 pint/600 ml vinegar*. Leave to steep for 2–3 weeks, then strain off the vinegar into bottles. Put a fresh sprig of the herb into each bottle – it looks attractive and adds extra strength to the vinegar.

HERB BUTTER

Soften *4 oz/125 g butter* with a fork, beat into it *a few drops of lemon juice* and *2–3 tablespoons of chopped herbs*. When the herbs and butter are well blended shape the butter into a roll, wrap it in foil and keep in the refrigerator until needed.

Herb butter can accompany grilled meat, poultry or fish and most vegetables and is good for making sandwiches.
The best herbs to flavour butter are basil, chives, dill, fennel, *fines herbes*, parsley, salad burnet and watercress.

TO CRYSTALLIZE BORAGE FLOWERS:

1 egg white
a handful of borage flowers
castor sugar

Beat the egg white until slightly frothy, then with a small brush paint it on both sides of the petals. Dip the flowers into a bowl of castor sugar, turning them over to make sure they are coated thoroughly. Spread them on an oven tray lined with greaseproof paper. On a warm day they will dry in the kitchen, otherwise put the tray into a low oven for 10 minutes, leaving the door open.

CLARET CUP

1 bottle claret
4 fl oz/125 ml cognac
3 tablespoons sugar
1 lemon, sliced, with peel
1 orange, sliced, with peel
10 crushed borage leaves
1 pint/600 ml soda water
borage leaves and flowers for garnish

Put the wine, cognac, sugar, fruit and borage in a large bowl and leave to stand for 2–3 hours, then chill thoroughly. To serve, strain into a large serving bowl, add soda water and ice cubes and float the flowers and leaves on the top.

I N D E X

ACKNOWLEDGEMENTS

*The publishers
would like to thank the
following people:*

· ILLUSTRATORS ·
JANE THOMSON
SHEILAGH NOBLE

JACKET
· PHOTOGRAPHY ·
PHILIP DOWELL

FALKINER FINE
PAPERS LTD

ALAN DAVIDSON

· TYPESETTING ·
WYVERN
TYPESETTING LTD

· REPRODUCTION ·
COLOURSCAN
SINGAPORE

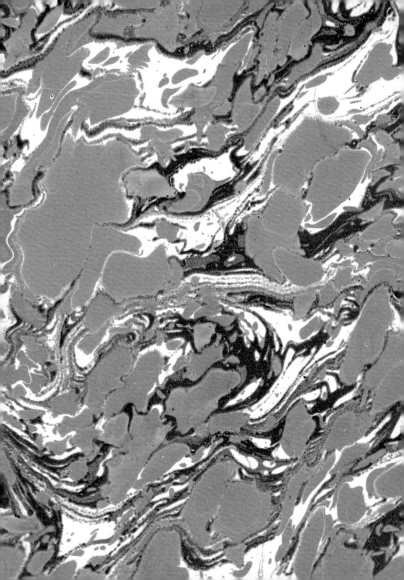